A Load of Old Bristle

Krek Waiter's Peak Bristle

Edited by Derek Robinson
With illustrations by Vic Wiltshire

COUNTRYSIDE BOOKS
NEWBURY BERKSHIRE

This omnibus edition first published 2002

COUNTRYSIDE BOOKS
3 Catherine Road,
Newbury, Berkshire.

ISBN 1 85306 792 X

Many thanks to Tony and Jane Osborne for photography; also to Colin Rose.

Designed by Derek Robinson and Peter Davies, Nautilus Design

Produced through MRM Associates Ltd, Reading

Printed by Woolnough Bookbinding Limited, Irthlingborough.

INTRODUCTION

'Sexual Depravity in Print!' shouted the headline in the Port Zed Gazette. 'We Expose the Textbook of Satanic Cults!' echoed the Bemster Bugle. 'Spelling Mistake on Page 4!' blasted the Times Educational Supplement. All corners of the mass media united against the first appearance of *Bristle*.

This has always been a city notorious for its sensitivity. Remember the shock-waves that made the Count's Louse tremble when Rovers went down 3-nil to Carlisle in a midweek friendly? So *Krek Waiter's Peak Bristle* came as a bombshell. Its revelation of the existence of an underground language – meaningless to foreigners from Scunthorpe, or even Severn Beach – rocked the citizens like no other scandal since the 1950s, when the Lady Mayoress, Grace Tepp-Ford, failed a sex-test and confessed that he was Stanley Grunge, a van driver from Shrampton.

After the attack by the tabloids came an orchestrated campaign to discredit Bristle. The English Department of Bristle University held a protest march from the Coronation Tap via the Greyhound to the Albion. There were riots in North Bristle University (formerly Sodding Chipbury Polytechnic) when the Chemistry Faculty tried to burn Derek Robinson in effigy but failed to achieve ignition.

Yet – like *Carmen* and *The Rites of Spring*, both savaged by the critics on opening night – *Krek Waiter's Peak Bristle* has survived the onslaught and become a popular icon, up there with the Clifton Suspension Bridge. Indeed, visitors often look at both the book and the bridge and ask, 'What keeps it up?' The answer, of course, is sheer charismal. Bristle is the city that put the L into charismal.

Derek Robinson

Derek Robinson

THE ARTIST

What can be said about Vic Wiltshire that hasn't been said a thousand times already?

Asked if he understood the bits of Bristle that Robinson wrote for the speech-bubbles, he was disarmingly modest. 'Gibberish, isn't it? Can't make head nor tail of it. Not English, that's for sure. Still, that's not my half of the job. I just write what he says and get on with the next illustration. But I sometimes wonder about young Derek. He played a lot or rugby, you know. Maybe he took too many knocks on the head. I like having him around, though. He makes the tea.'

Bristle is in Vic Wiltshire's blood; he was born and bred here. He has no idea where his artistic brilliance came from. 'It's like falling off a bicycle,' he explains. 'Either you can do it or you can't. Mind you, it's never easy. I practised for years. Rome wasn't burned in a day, remember.'

Asked if he could sum up the secret of his long and successful partnership with Robinson, Vic thought hard and finally said: 'He can't draw and I can't write. Now get out of my way. I'm going to play golf.' And off he went.

EUREKAL!

The famous Bristle L

Bristle is the only city in Britain to be able to turn ideas into ideals, areas into aerials, and Monicas into monocles.

Nobody knows why the Bristle folk slap an L on the end of any and every word which offers a conveniently overhanging 'a' or 'o' sound, but they do, and it's been going on for a long time. 'Bristle' itself was made out of brig (bridge) and stowe (place) plus a final L to keep the dust out.

Probably the most famous result of the Bristle L was the city father who had three lovely daughters, Idle, Evil and Normal. (To these can be added three other uniquely Bristle girls: Annal, Martial and Monocle.) But without a doubt the most telling demonstration of the Bristle L took place some years ago when a television crew recorded several citizens while they read aloud the words on a theatre poster, which turned out to be featuring Eval Turner, Primal Donnal of the Carl Rosal Operal. It goes without saying that the company performed such works as Aidal, La Traviatal, Rigolettol, and Cavalerial Rusticanal.

Few foreign countries are safe from the Bristle L. It ranges the world, from Nigerial to Malaysial, from Bolivial to Americal, from Costal Rical to the Costal Braval. It affects Canadal and Austrialial (for which you need a visal) as well as the notorious malarial areal of Africal.

But it is in everyday life that the Bristle L flourishes. A local girl who was learning to dance was heard to say, 'I can rumble but I can't tangle.' Bristle housewives go shopping for bananals, semolinal, tinned tunal fish, and a Victorial sandwich, as well as Ryvital and Ambrosial creamed rice. Kitchen tops are covered with Formical. Sinks are cleaned with ammonial.

Hardly anything in the garden escapes – begonials, fuschials, dahlials, hydrangeals, even aspidistrals. And not even diseases are immune. People in Bristle have been struck down by the grisly influenzal and pneumonial. Happily, diphtherial is rare, although visitors should beware the dreaded Dire Eel.

Neither television nor religion offers any escape from the Bristle L. You're just as likely to find yourself watching Panoramal, or Delial Smith, or a programme from Granadal. And if you go to church, it will probably turn out to be either St Brendal's, St Helenal's or St Teresal's.

You can always get in your car and drive away, of course. Just make sure it isn't a Hondal, Toyotal, Alfal-Romeol, Volvol, etceteral, etceteral, etceteral.

Aft Trawl: Taking everything into account; as in: 'Less walk - aft trawl snot far, anna rains topped.'

Add Lessons: Teenagers.

Aerial: District or region. If you get bad radio or TV reception, don't blame the set. Blame the aerial.

Am Rim: Cry uttered by spectators at Rugby match whenever opponent gets the ball.

Angry Neighed: Small bombshell.

Annie's Cord: Triumphant exclamation by football commentator.

Annual: Start of a promise; as in: 'Butcher specks on, annual see much fervour.'

Annuity: Claim to insight; as in: 'Annuity was line, cuzzy turn dread.'

Annum: Part of Bristle, near Mangusfeel. Site of Roman transit camp; hence the expression 'Per Annum', meaning 'Change at Staleton Road'.

Ant Chew Erred: News intro; as in: 'Ant chew erred? Lass train scone, ten mince ago.'

Ant Eye: Appeal for support, usually tacked on to end of sentence; as in: 'Core sigh can't goat the pitchers. Gotta state tome an mine the baby, ant eye?'

Ant Senior: Opening remark of reunion; as in: 'Ant senior furlong time'.

Ardour: Less soft.

Ark Tim: Never heard such rubbish.

Armagh: Mum.

Armchair: Question meaning 'What do they cost?' as in: 'Armchair yer eat napples, mister?'

Arry V. Dirt Cheap: Farewell until we meet again. Being a seaport, Bristle has adopted many foreign phrases and given them a local twist as they settled into the rich compost which is West Country dialect. For instance, the all-purpose exclamation 'Blige', heard only in Bristle, is a corruption of the Old French *bel liege*, meaning Good Lord, which was the sort of thing they said in Bordeaux when told that Rovers had lost to Carlisle.

Arry V. Dirt Cheap comes from 'Arry's Bar in Naples, where the price of drinks was low but their octane rating was high. Visiting seamen said that a visit to 'Arry's Bar meant a swift goodbye to consciousness. They took the phrase back to Bristle. Today, long after the bar and its owner have been forgotten, men still make their farewells with the Neapolitan cry, 'Arry V. Dirt Cheap!'

Ashen Core: Former stately home, still standing in rolling parkland near Long Ashen.

Avenue: Question expecting negative answer; as in: 'Avenue kids gotcher closon yet?'

Awry: Reluctant agreement; as in: 'Awry, awry, avitcherone way.'

Bart Nil: Area of Bristle between Reckliff and Lorne's Ill.

Beers Port: Play fair. Ancient chant, traditionally uttered by the natives in order to bring about a change of fortune. Rarely successful.

Beet Root Chew: Declaration of faithfulness; as in: 'I'll always beet root chew, luv.'

Bell Tup: Less of your lip.

Bem Breckfuss: Form of toll or tribute extorted from outsiders passing through the district. Similar to 'Overnight Accommodation', which costs £5 more.

Bess Tie Can: Don't expect more.

Biff: Portion of; as in: 'Gissa biff your bren jam.'

Bill Tup: Urban area.

Bind: Not in front.

Bind Jew: To your rear.

Bit Rend: Unpleasant outcome.

Bleed Nell!: Exclamation of shock or dismay.

Bleed Nero: Term used in recognition of outstanding sporting activity; as in: 'Ease plain Leica bleed Nero.'

Blige: Untranslatable term, used to indicate emphasis or emotion; as in 'Blige, Bert, bleed knot, knit?'

Blood Yell: Exclamation of surprise.

Blow: Underneath. Opposite of **Buv.**

Blow Defy: Haven't got a clue. I give up; as in: 'Blow defy know.'

NINCH DOWN... TWINGES UP...LESSEN THAT...LIL BIT TRITE...CAN CHEW STAN STILL FOR TOMB MINCE?
CAN CHEWER FORD A LONGER CHAIN, FOR PEACE ACHE?
SORDID DOUBT! SCOLD!

Bomb: The lowest level; as in: 'They mussby scrapin bomb the barrel, thassall icon say.'

Bone Narrows: Archery.

Brand Nil: High point overlooking the centre of Bristle, giving good views of Bemminster, Smary Reckliff and parts of Comm, as well as the Float Narbor.

Brassy Air: Underwear with uplift.

Bren Jam: Popular food item.

Bristle: Commercial, industrial and cultural centre of the West. Bristle has a rich social life. Two examples, chosen at random, are: *Bristle Am Chewer Pratick Sigh Tea,* and *Bristle Rovers Sporters Sigh Tea.* Others occur throughout these pages.

Bristle Grams Cool: Local academy for boys.

Buffer: Had circumstances been otherwise; as in: 'Buffer rim, she'd bean side a nurse gnome now.'

Bum Tinto: Met by chance; as in: 'Guess why bum tinto in Shrampton smorning?'

Butcher: Invitation to take part; as in: 'Butcher self in mice use, Harry.'

Butcher Tea Fin: Replace your dentures.

But Knoll: Small slit in clothing.

Cadaver: Expression of possibility; as in: 'We cadaver week's holly daze necks yer.'

Can Chew: Irritated challenge of inability; as in: 'Can chew stan still?'

Canteen: Measure of extreme inability; as in: 'Fat? He canteen seize zone feet knee more!'

Cantilever: Criticism of male intentions; as in: 'Cantilever alone for five mince?'

SUP CHEW, KNIT? WEAKEN HAVE PINE CHIPS, OR SCRAMBLE DECKS, BUT CHORE NOT COME NIN LOOKING LEICA RUB SHEEP.
MITE SWELL GOAT THE PUB...
FIE COME, WILLY BIAS A PINT?

Car Key: Army brown.

Carnation: Climax of local beauty contest, as the winner gets crowned.

Carnival: Warning against greed; as in: 'Yer, you carnival them straw breeze!'

Cease: Chairs.

Cess Rees: Extra items, e.g. gloves, handbags, earrings, etc. Sometimes known as 'Matching cess rees', which cost 25% more.

Chess: Upper part of body, e.g. Chess eggs ray.

Chews Dee: Follows Monday.

Chuck Doubt: Expelled.

Claps: Fall to pieces.

Clift Nice Cool: Bristle's answer to Roedean.

Clyde: Run into.

Coal Snaw: Large building near the centre of Bristle, used for wrestling and symphony concerts.

Comm: Section of Bristle between Red Lun, Snandroos and Brand Nil.

Connive: Request for something; as in: 'Connive me pock-money?'

Corn Twim: In his opinion.

Corsairs; Corsets: These words usually introduce a confident claim, such as: 'Corsairs moron one waiters kin a cat.'
Or: 'Corsets knotter real usban, juno.'

Count's Louse: Large building below Brand Nil, containing the offices of local government. Also small buildings inhabited by ratepayers.

ON SLEE !
SIX MUNCE INTO LONG.
VERAL ! YUKON BUTCHER TEA FINNAN SAY 'ARRY V. DIRT CHEAP' CHORE MUM. SHE SNOT STAIN YEARN KNEE LONGER !
LISTEN TOMB ! ALWAYS AT LOG REDS !

Course: Musical term, e.g. dawn course; course girl; all join in the course.

Cue: Questions ability; as in: 'Cue see pasture nose?'

Dane Age: The era in question; the way things are; as in: 'Stimey got married - aft trawl, ease twenny-sem. Snot natural, knottin this dane age.'

Dan Saul: Enclosed area where deafening music is played while customers agitate themselves opposite each other. The performance may or may not be concluded with a punch-up.

Daze: Measurements of time.

Deaf Knit: Positive, certain, guaranteed; as in: 'Lens a quid - lav it back Wensdee, deaf knit.'

Deck Rating: Painting and wallpapering.

Dennis: Tooth doctor.

Diesel: Introductory threat; as in: 'Diesel get my fist up thy frote.' When the fist itself is displayed, the threat may be shortened to 'Diesel getty.'

Din Chew, Din Twee: Used for questions expecting positive answers. **Din Chew** is often used aggressively, as in: 'Maida nidgetcher self genn lass night, din chew?' In contrast, **Din Twee** usually assumes total harmony; as in: 'Bert nye haddock rate big room altar selves, din twee, Bert?'

Dire Eel: Loose tubes.

FEWER THE CUP LOO ORDERED MACK RULL, COOK SEX STREAM LEA SORRY, BUTTER CAT SCONE AN SCOFF DIT.
VET SCUM. CORN TWIM, CATTLE BE WELLA GAIN IN TOUR FREE DAZE.
GUESS A SAM WITCH, DEN.
SAM WITCHES ROFF, LUV.

Doom:	A telescoping of 'do' and either 'him' or 'them'. People urging the return of National Service say it would 'doom' a power of good.
Door:	Female child.
Dorne Lore:	Wife of male child.
Double Dover:	Completely bent.
Doughnut Tempt:	Forget it. You'll fail.
Dummy:	Phrase meaning 'completed by'; as in: 'Tell meal laughter wait – I can't seam till eye dummy pools.'
Duns:	Groups of twelve.
Dunt:	Signifies failure; as in: 'Saviour breath – he dunt know.'

SMATTER?
SONY HARPS TWO.
SNOW GOOD...
EYE MUSTER GOT
INSOMNIAL.
EYE SHUNT OF HAD THAT
TINNER BEANS STRAY TAFTER
TENNER LEAVEN PINTSA
BIT RAIL.
GNAT CASE, ICE
PECKED YULE HAVE
DIRE EEL TOO.

Dwight Elm Outer: Start of retaliatory remark tinged with indignation; as in: 'Wine tea mined zone business? Aft trawl, dwight elm outer do *is* job?'

Earner: Expression of feminine contempt; as in: 'Ooze she kidding wither big eye deals? Earner count's louse!'

Ease Add: Record of share distribution; as in: 'Snot fair – ease add moron me.'

Ease Poster: Allegation of responsibility; as in: 'Ease poster get the gross rees, not me.'

East Dregs: Highly coloured chocolate confections, eaten in the spring.

Een Pos: One of two newspapers serving Bristle and district. The other is the **Wessunday Press.** They are easily

distinguishable: the **Wessunday Press** carries stories about fires, floods and football, and luridly scandalous court cases in outlying parts of the West Country such as Kings Lynn, Glasgow and Scunthorpe; whereas the **Een Pos** carries stories about fires, floods and football, and up to 14 solid pages of classified advertising.

Embree: Suburb of Bristle, between Lorne's Wessun and Wesbree.

Eva Narder: Patron saint of Bristle. Her name is invoked for support and encouragement whenever failure threatens, as in: 'Snow good give nup – try Eva Narder.' Also: 'They played hard, but we played Eva Narder.'

Ev Smuch: A great deal, a lot. **Ev S'** is the universal term of emphasis in Bristle. For example, 'Ev Sgood' means anything from

'not bad' to 'fantastic'. Other Ev-words are: Ev Snice, Ev Seasy, Ev Soften, Ev Sot, Ev Scold, Ev Sweat, Ev Slate, Ev Sold and Ev Sevvy.

Evil: Girl's name.

Excise: P.T.

Eye Mustard: Self-justification. See also: **Mustard Old Jew.**

Eye Shunt: That's where I went wrong.

Fairy Nuff: Expression of satisfaction, based on the well known passion of the Little Folk for British justice. (For the benefit of those unfamiliar with the world of elves and pixies, Fairy Nuff was the one in Enid Blyton with red hair and freckles, who was victimised when Noddy circulated false rumours of drunkenness and shoplifting and had her hounded out of the Union. It was in all the papers.)

FOR
PEACE ACHE!
ANT CHEW GONNY CENTS?
SNOT MORON TOMB MINCE SIN SIGH
FINCHED DOONE THIS FLORA GAIN!
TAY COUGH YER MUCKY DAPS!
MICE SOCK
SERENE MUCKIER.

Fall Go Swell: Hoping for the best.

Fans Stress: Exotic costume.

Fax: Data.

Fee: Opening of suggestion, as in: 'Fee cries, gimmis boll.' Similar openings are **Fie, Few** and **Fitz**, as in:
'Fie scene, I'll punchiz teefin.'
'Few wannum, better pay forum.'
'Fitz wet, I'm stain omen watchin telly.'

Fervour: Greater distance; as in: 'Can't go knee fervour – summonse dug up the road.'

Feud: Beginning of suggestion; as in: 'Feud shrup a mint, you'd seat eye mean.' A similar opening is **Fuel**; as in: 'Fuel grout an shove, I'll stain side and steer.'

Fight Old Jew: Hint of remarkable revelations; as in: 'Fight old jew hooey stake nowt, ewed beam azed.'

Fig Red: Statue at sharp end of ship.

Finch: End; as in: 'Ant chew finched yet?'

Fine: Discover.

Flat List: Stamp collector.

Flup: No room.

Forced Dean: Large wooded area in Gloucestershire.

Ford: Opposite of backward.

Foreign: With another person in mind; as in: 'Ussle wait foreign ear.'

Forgots Ache: Kindly give me your undivided attention.

Fought: Considered.

Four Stout: Ejected by force; as in this typical piece of Rugby commentary: '. . . annie nearly scores butties four stout'.

Four Stranger: Keeper of woodland.

Freeze A Bird: Completely at liberty.

Fuel: Offer of co-operation; as in 'Fuel go to Sanes Breeze, I'll make summit tweet.'

Furze: To an extent; as in: 'Saul overrun dunwith, furze icon see.'

Genny; Gonny: These interchangeable words are widely used to introduce an inquiry concerning the availability of items or objects.

Genny is used where a third party has been involved in the transaction; e.g. 'Genny good books uppa lye bree?' On the other hand, **Gonny** is used for direct questioning: 'Gonny thin teat? Gonny threench nails? Gonny sisters tome?'

Geronwy: See **Stain**.

Ghost Ark Raven Mad: Behave oddly.

Ghost Ray Tome: What to do after school.

Ginger: Start of question concerning wellbeing; as in:
A. 'Scold out smornin – Ice lipped onna payment.'
B. 'Ginger yourself?'

Giraffe: Plea for more considerate behaviour; as in:
'Bleed Nell – giraffe to take up all the bed?'

Gloss Trode: Shopping area and highway leading north out of Bristle.

Gnashed Ray: For dog-ends.

Gnat Case: In those circumstances.

Gnome: Claim acquaintance with; as in: 'Gnome? Coarse eye gnome! We bin mace for munce!'

Gob Less: Benediction, invariably said at the parting of two or more Bristle people, perhaps when one of them is leaving for foreign parts, such as Sodding Chipbury, or Nempnett Thrubwell, or even (Heaven help us) Peasedown St John. On occasions like these, and at times of extreme peril, such as the visit of Millwall fans to Ashton Gate, the good folk of Bristle put their affairs in order, bury their silver in the back garden, and call upon Providence to protect them, using the age-old words: 'Gob Less.' The phrase originated in the Black Death of 1348. We know now that this plague was bubonic fever, brought to Bristle by hordes of black rats from Milton Keynes, or it might have been Bognor Regis; anyway, somewhere in Essex. Various futile cures were attempted. One of the most popular required the patient to spit over his (or her) left shoulder. If anything, this helped to spread the infection. Eventually the plague burnt itself out, which just proved that spitting over the left shoulder really worked. The fact that they no longer needed to do it led the survivors to remind each other of their good luck. 'Gob Less,' they said. Six centuries later, the salutation has become extended to all forms of danger, including trying to get off the M5 at Avonmouth.

Gorgeous: Inevitable remark by visitors to Clifton, as in: 'The gorgeous bewful, innit?'

Grace Tepp-Ford: Bristle's First Lady, and an essential figure in all public works. Her name is hailed to justify spending the taxpayers' money on everything from bigger roundabouts (distributing the traffic jams so that everybody gets a bit) to computerised crematoria (despatching us to eternity with split-second efficiency). Hardly a municipal speech goes by without some reference to her: 'Before declaring this Sewage Treatment Works open, I should like to congratulate the citizens of Bristle on another Grace Tepp-Ford.' In her time, Mrs Tepp-Ford has been associated with many notable events in Bristle. The Brabazon was a Grace Tepp-Ford. Broadmead

WOSS
SCOT, MUM?
BLOW DEFY REMEMBER!
SALES ARE BET RUN LAST
CHEER! STUNS A BARGAINS!
EYE WRECK NIGH SAVIOUR
DAD MORON ICE PENT!
BLEED NELL!
WORSE TALL
GONE?

shopping centre was a Grace Tepp-Ford. There was a report that the recent modernisation and improvement of the Bristle bus services was yet another Grace Tepp-Ford and, judging by the number of people to be seen walking home, that's probably right.

Grain: Turning grey.

Grape Ride: Much self-esteem.

Grape Written: England, Ireland, Scotland and Wales. The S.S. Grape Written is in dry dock in Bristle.

Greyful: Appreciative. Moron Greyful: Highly appreciative.

Groan Pains: Childhood discomfort.

Gross Rees: Household goods sold in, e.g., the supermarket.

Grout: See **Less.**

Guard Nose: Horticultural equipment.

Guess: Please supply me with; as in: 'Guess a beer, luv.'

Guess Tuck Interim: Urgent encouragement to greater effort, usually heard at football matches.

Guise: See **Scouse.**

Hard Tack: Cardiac failure.

Harps: Thirty minutes past the hour.

Holly Daze: Vacations.

Homer Bout: Estimated time of arrival.

Honest Ale: Close behind. Police jargon, frequently used in *The Bill*: 'Keep honest ale, McCann. Watchim Leica nawk.'

I Cadaver: It would be possible for me to have a ...

Ice Pecked: Suggest a likelihood; as in: 'Ice pecked ease gone infra beer.'

Ice Pose: **Ice Poseys**; **Ice Poser**: Suggest a possibility, as in: 'Snot on telly, ice pose?' 'Ice poseys gone wafer is holly daze.' 'Ice poser dad wooden letter seam again.'

Idle: Girl's name.

Incher: Challenge; as in: 'Drinkin my scrumpy, incher?'

Infra: Imminent experience, usually painful; as in: 'Ease infra shock.'

Instant: Happening, event.

Intense: Under canvas.

Into: Not very; as in: 'She into good at sums, butter jogger free slot better.'

Isolate: Indicates reluctance to act; as in: 'Isolate moon away from Bristle. Aft trawl, swear I grup, innit?'

Jeer: This is one of two words widely used in conversation to draw attention to items of news. **Jeer** refers to news transmitted by the spoken word. An example of its use is:
'Jeer onna news poster rain all necks munf?'
'Jeer bout Stan come nup onna Pools? Won fortify quid.'
'Jeer er-necks-door go non bout R bonfire downa bomba garn? Sedditz smoky nupper washin.' For reference to news transmitted visually, see **Sauna**.

Jew Asbestos: Expression of disbelief; as in: 'Jew asbestos bleev that?'

Jiminez: Expression of masculine contempt; as in: 'Jiminez (pronounced Himiniz) big ideals.' The feminine equivalent is **Earner**.

Jogger Fee: Sea, countries, mountains, rivers, and all that stuff.

Jubilee: Question of opinion; as in: 'Jubilee view should stake wyatt? Or jubilee vince pekin your mine?'

Juggler: Big vein in the neck.

Juicy: Word used to introduce an inquiry about something taking place, as in:
'Juicy what icy?'
Or 'Juicy the nude reins been laid inna necks treat?'

Justice Swell: Expression of right and proper behaviour; as in: 'No, we dingo way, we stay dome. Justice swell – trained all week.'

Knee: Key to general enquiry; as in: 'See knee M.T. cease?'
'Bring knee thin treed?'

Knocked Puss: Eight suckers. It's actually a mollusc, same as an oyster. Look it up, if you don't believe me.

Krek: Accurate; as in: 'Krek time squaw pass sen.'

Kwor: Four ounces.

Lady Slavs: Half of a public convenience.

Lass: Final.

Lass Cheer: Memories, memories.

EASE PULLIN MY PINT, ANNIE SEZ, 'LOOK SLY CRANE' TWITCH EYE SEZ, LEICA FLASH, 'DONT TAY SLY CREEL BEER EITHER' AN OLIVER SUN, I'M CHUCK DOUBT!
The SPOTTED COW
WODGE YEW SPECK? EASE SCOT NO CENSOR YUMA!

Lass Mint: Very late; urgent.

Late Ron: Not yet.

Lav: Note of urgency or compulsion; as in: 'Lav turry - slate.' 'Lav towarder writ, luv, snottin stock.'

Lay Bricks Change: Job Centre.

Lay Tron: In due course; as in: 'Sid seddy might poppin lay tron. Stimey did – ease eddied beer yes-day.'

Lean Tomb: Recommendation of non-interference; as in: 'Yer! You lean tomb self, rile beacher red in !' A similar phrase is **Lean Lone**; as in: 'That paint sweat – lean lone!'

Lecher: Permissive advice; as in: 'Wine chew guess tuck into the scrumpy, an lecher rare down?'

Leica Flash: Rapidly.

Less: Proposal of action; as in: 'Swarm near, knit? Less grout.' Or: 'Less bailey tout – scotta lotta wart rinse ide.'

Lessee: Note of caution; as in:
A. 'Started train – we might swell goat the pitchers.'
B. 'Well, lessee fits gonny buddy good knit, first.'

Less Fey Sit: We might as well accept the facts.

Less Packet Tin: I suggest we stop.

Levi Loan: Plea for personal privacy. In Bristle it is often accompanied by the warning: 'Or diesel feel my fist.'

Libel: Likely or inclined; as in: 'Coal Snaw's libel to be soul doubt.'

Lice: Illuminations. These take many forms, such as Head Lice.

Lice Witch: Device for controlling lice.

Limp Picks: Top athletes making heroic efforts not to get caught by the drug testers.

Line: Dishonest; as in: 'Ease line, yeronner!'

Log Reds: Deadlock.

Lonely Bee: Understatement, as in: 'Yukon stain a car few like - lonely bee fie mince.' Or:
'Jew wanna comfortee? It lonely bee bren jam, ice pecked.'

Lorne's Ill: District of Bristle situated in Up Reaston. It lies between Bart Nil, Staleton Road, and the Riv Raven.

Loss: Large quantities; plenty.

Mace: Friends.

Major: Reflection on some other person's behaviour, as in: 'Ant chew major mine dup yet?'

Mangus Feel: Rural community to the north-east of Bristle.

Mansh Nowce: Lord Mayor's residence.

May Doubter: Constructed from.

McNubbout: Many words owe their origins to surnames. 'Hooligan' came from a delinquent Irish family in London, the O'Hulihans. The Earl of Sandwich invented the packed lunch, Wellington gave us the boot, and it was a Brighton greengrocer (and amateur inventor) by the name of W. C. Flush who perfected the modern toilet; while we owe the word 'harass' to a notoriously persistent rent-collector in 18th century Lancashire, one Zebedee Harris. Bristle's contribution to this list comes from a Scottish kilt-manufacturer, Hamish McNubbout (1753 – 1829) who came south and established a business in Reckliff. Demand for kilts in that part of Bristle was slight, and Hamish McNubbout found himself with so much time on his hands that eventually his name became a byword for idling. When asked by their parents what they had been up to, kids used to mumble: 'Juss McNubbout.' In those days they usually got a clip on the ear for not speaking properly.

Might Swell: For all the difference it makes.

Mike Cod: Goodness gracious me.

Mill: Centre.

Mimi: Rendezvous instructions; as in: 'Mimi outside the Count's Louse.'

Mince: Short periods of time. See also **Munce**.

Mine: Intellect.

Mine Jew: Take into account.

Miniature: The very instant; no sooner than; as in: 'Miniature back sterned, summonse upto summit.'

Mint: Sixty seconds.

Miracle: USA. Cabot discovered a Miracle in 1497.

Miss Tree: Something unexplained.

LIST NEAR – FEW DON'T GUESS MORE EXCISE, YOU'LL GROPE SHORTEN FATTEN SIR VIEW RIGHT, GNAW.
BURP?

Moat Wrist: Road user.

Moff: Statement of departure; as in: 'Moff to Scouse now, dad-connive me pock-money?'

Moira Wave Life: Whenever the citizens of Bristle find the plain, unvarnished truth a bit of a strain on the eyeballs, they call in Moira Wave-Life to refurbish the facts and create a more glamorous image. Miss Wave-Life runs a Public Relations agency which is so successful that the very sound of her name is enough to transform the dullest activity into an exciting, rewarding crusade. 'Pickled eggs,' declares a typical press release from her agency, ' are not so much an industry – Moira Wave-Life.'

Monocle: Girl's name. St Monocle's is a palatial retirement home.

Moron: Greater than. A common expression of thanks is: 'I'm moron greyful.'

Munce: Long periods of time. See also **Mince**.

Muse Call: Old-fashioned entertainment, killed off by telly, which in turn is so terrible that old-fashioned Muse Call has now been revived, called Stand-Up Comedy.

Mustard Old Jew: Frequent repetition; as in: 'Eye mustard old jew hundreds of times...'

My Loud: Request for permission; as in: 'My loud to eat my East dregs?'

Myrrh: Looking-glass.

Nab Salute, A: A complete and utter.

Natchafack: To tell the truth; in reality; as in: 'Saul lies, yerronner! Natchafack I nev reeven touch dim – he mustard riven into a waller summit.'

Neck Store: Neighbouring.

Ness Serry: What's needed. Anything that's tzar bull but not absolutely sensual is ness serry.

Neuter: Unfamiliar with; as in:
A. 'How dye getta Gloss Trode?'
B. 'Dunno, I'm neuter Bristle.'

Nev Reeven: See **Natchafact**.

Nice Cool: Evening institute.

Nigh: Plaintive ending of defensive statement; as in:
'Av nart – I'm doona bess-eye can, nigh?'
'Woss speck – I only got one pair vands, nigh?'

Ninch: Very short distance. See also **Twinges**.

Normal: Girl's name.

Nose Snot: Negative reply; as in:
A. 'Din ronna table yet?'
B. 'Nose snot.'

Now Daze: At present.

Numb Rate: Between 7 and 9.

Nurse Gnome: Kind of high-class hospital. Good place to recover from a claps.

Office Ed: Daft. The original Office Ed was a clerk named Edward Upjohn, who worked in a Chinese spaghetti factory in Bemmister. People used to get drunk and telephone him in the middle of the night, saying: 'Are you up, John?' It drove him daft.

Oliver Sun: Unexpectedly.

On Slee: Actually; in truth. Often used for emphasis, with a ! thrown in for good measure; as in: 'So I said, "Lissen," I said, "woss mean?" I said. Annie sediment watty said, from the bomb is art. On slee!'

Ooze Necks?: Phrase chanted by Bristle shopkeepers. Even if you're the only person in the shop, they still say, 'Ooze necks?' They like to be in command.

Ooze Pain?: Query about source of money.

Ooze Pekin?: What people say when they answer the phone. They really want to know your name, but they're afraid to ask.

Pain Guess: Posh boarder.

Pains Tones: Stumbling blocks laid on the pavement. In wet weather they rock, and squirt dirty water up your legs.

Pasture: This way; as in: 'Scene knee numb rate buses go pasture?'

Payment: Sidewalk; as in: 'Stain a payment – you'll get knock dover'.

Peace Ache, For: Expression of impatience. Less intense then **Forgots Ache**.

Phoney: Wishful thinking; as in:
A. 'Phoney I cud grow brockley biggs yorn, Bert. Woss put on un?'
B. 'Scald "The Mixture", Sid. Wife gessit frommer doctor. Dunt doer chess knee good, but it dough-naff bring on my brockley, loik.'

Pine Chips: Simple grub, improved by plenty of brown sauce. Popular with café society. Others include Scramble Decks and Saucy Jeggan Chips.

Plain: Taking part in organised sport; as in:
A. 'Wisey plain sent-raff?'
B. 'Avenue erred? Reggler sent-raffs busty sand.'

Plain Feels: Sports grounds.

Plea Scar: Panda.

Plover: Kind of sweater.

Port Zed: Coastal town opposite Avemouth. The Macao of the West.

Prayed: March-past.

Puncher: Flat tyre.

Ray-Joe Bristle: Local broadcasting station with two DJs, Ray Gin-Eddake and Joe Kinnapart.

Ree's Knees: Explanation; as in: 'Ree's knees fed up scuzzies onny zone, C.'

Relay: Emphatic response indicating mild astonishment; as in:
A. 'Ant chew erred? Easy loped wither from neck store!'
B. 'No! Relay?'

Reporse: Newspaper stories.

Rifle: Deserving. Prince Charles is the Rifle Air.

Rice: Entitlements; as in: 'Book 'im an' read 'im 'is rice.'

Rival: Entry.

Rub Sheep: Pile of garbage.

Rumble: South American dance. See also **Tangle**.

Sam Witch: Fast food.

Sane: Expression, proverb; as in Old Country Sane, and Sane of the Week.

Sanes Breeze: Supermarket.

Sarong Place: We should be elsewhere.

Sartnoon: Later on today.

Sauna: Word used extensively in conversation to draw attention to items of news. **Sauna** refers to news transmitted in pictures; for instance:
'Sauna telly lass night bout all them forced fires nosstralia.'
'Sauna news they got jam surround X-ter gain. Sauls the same, knit?' See also **Jeer**.

Scampi: Statement of impossibility; as in: 'This scampi wary lives – scot no lice on.'

Scars: Cylinders of tobacco, reputedly a damn good smoke.

Scene Sow: Under the prevailing conditions; as in: 'Scene sow ease always onna beer, snow under he puss on smuch weight.'

Scold: Evidence of the white-hot pace of intellectual ferment in Bristle is the ability of its citizens to use only one word to communicate complex ideas which require several words elsewhere in the country.
Scold (The weather is not as warm as it might be) is an example. Others are:
Scum (It has arrived)
Slate (It has not arrived)
Snot (I am afraid you have miscalculated)
Snow? (Are you aware of what I have revealed to you?)
Snuff (That is quite sufficient)
Surly (It has arrived ahead of time)
Swarm near (This room is noticeably hot)
Stun (The project has been completed)

BLOOD YELL !
SCENE THIS?
EARN NECK STORE
SCONE ANNIE LOPED
WITHER PAIN GUESS !
EASE STAR CRAVEN !
SHE STUFFER THAN
FORMICAL ! INSIDE A
NURSE GNOME, SWEAR
EEL LEND UP !

You will see from this list that it is possible in Bristle to conduct a valuable exchange of views while using only a handful of words. Here are two Bristolians discussing the End of the World:
A. Scum!
B. Snot, snow. Slate.
A. No, scum. Surly. Sought meself.
B. (Furiously) Snot! Snot! Slate!
A. (Curiously) Smatter?
B. (Brokenly) Snout . . . Swarm near . . . (Whispering) Sure scum?
A. Scum, awry. Saul over. (PAUSE) Scold out.
B. Swarm near, though. Snuff, knit?
A. Snuff? Sample! (PAUSE, THEN QUIETLY:) Scum. On slee.
B. (SIGHS HEAVILY) Stun . . .

Scone: It's not here any more.

Scone Chord!: Cry uttered in Bristle when supersonic aircraft flies overhead.

Scouce: See **Guise**.

Scum: It's here.

Seedy: Much of the rich fabric of life in Bristle is the result of constant contact – people recognising each other, and recognising that they themselves have, in turn, been recognised. The codeword **Seedy** is invaluable for this exchange, and it is heavily used. For instance:
A. Seedy uppa Rovers, Sat-dee.
B. Ah? Dint C.D., though. Whirr bouts wast?
A. Bind a goal.
B. Oh, ah. Yer, seedy gotten gaged, den! Zinna paper wonnit?
A. R. Genn marred up Smarys, prolly.

Seizure: It's not so difficult; as in: 'One shoe guess tarted, seizure knit looks.'

Senior: Start of personal enquiry; as in: 'Senior dad knee wear? Ease poster mimi yer quart van our ago.'

Sensual: Vital, crucial; as in: 'Snot juss ness serry – sab slootly sensual.' See also **Ness Serry**.

Sentry: 100 years.

Serfs: The outside area.

Shane Cream; Shane Soap: Male toiletries.

Shleedown: Residential area of Bristle, near Snandroos.

Short Urn: You're next.

Shrampton: Another residential area of Bristle, between Lorne's Wessun and Avemouth.

Shunt: Not a good idea; as in: 'You shunt picket, or it'll never get better.'

Sickle Downer: Nauseated; as in: 'R Normal went honour Sunny's Cool out-in yesdee, and she was sickle downer teacher's plover.'

Sikh Debts: Teenage sailors.

FORGOTS ACHE! DOUGHNUT TEMPTER SHUT KNEE GATES BIND JEW! SHEEP PROLLY WANT SOME HOLLY DAZE! ANJOU SLOP TALL MIKE COFFEE.
ARK TIM! DOONE THE BESS TIE CAN! BELL TUP, RILE DO MORON SLOPPIT - ISLE DUMB PIT!

Sill Sernt: Government employee.

Sin: Not standing. Sin room: place where tea is served on Sundays.

Sinew: Reported sighting; as in: 'I sinew with Normal lass tweek, dint I?'

Sink Ready Bull: I don't believe it.

Sit, Knit?: Nothing more to be said.

Skewer Tea: Freedom from anxiety; confidence; as in: 'Pay saul right, butties got no skewer tea.'

Skills: Pub game.

Smary Reckliff: What visitors mistake for Bristle Cathedral.

Smatter?: Something wrong?

Smite Urn: I'm next.

Snandroos: Part of Bristle, not far from Red Lun.

Snanz: Another part of Bristle, between Lorne's Ill and Annum. It lies in a bend of the Riv Raven.

Snot: Stout denial.

Snow: You know.

Snow Good: It's useless. Not to be confused with **Snow Under** (I'm not surprised) or **Snow**? (tacked onto the end of any statement to prevent the meaning leaking out).

Sod: How curious.

Sony: That's all it is. It isn't any more.

Sordid Doubt: Cleared up, explained; as in: 'Snot my pigeon, squire, sup chew to get it sordid doubt.'

Soul Doubt: None left.

Sparky: Snot ott.

Speckle: Statement of intent; as in: 'Speckle gopher a beer afterwards.' Speckle is derived from **Speck**. See also **Wodge**.

Spine: Espionage.

Sporse: Organised games, usually conducted on plain feels. People who attend sporse but don't take part are known as sporters.

Sporse Scar: Loud and uncomfortable means of transportation. Usually does 12 miles to the gallon. Insurance premiums for sporse scars are calculated by multiplying the maximum speed by 5 and adding 250 if the driver is an actor, a student, a professional sporseman, or under 65.

Stain: Don't go out; as in: 'Moff to bingo – yew stain Geronwy yer Romework.'

Stans Treason: Commonsense indicates.

Star Craven Mad: Mildly eccentric if rich. Dangerously irresponsible if poor.

Star Tin Train: The fine weather has broken.

Stay Plill: District of Bristle, on the way to Mangus Feel.

Stiff Cut: Diploma.

Stiff Runt: It's not the same.

Story Cheaters: Way of keeping the house warm.

Stray Ford: Simple, honest, uncomplicated.

Stray Tafter: Without delay.

Stream Lee: Very much so.

Strew: That's right.

Stuns: There's lots of.

Sup Chew Knit: Passing the buck. For example:

'Waddle eye sate rim, fee guess fresher summit?'

'Sup chew, knit?'

Sum Set: Neighbouring county.

Summer: A particular place.

Summer Thurr: More or less in that direction.

Summit: A particular thing.

Summon: A particular person.

Sunny's Cool: Bible class for the young.

Surly; Surlier; Surliest: These are all statements of time. **Surly** means it's ahead of time. **Surlier** means it's even further ahead. **Surliest** means it's so far ahead that nothing can catch it.

Swat; Swear: Everyday declarations of fact. **Swat** tells you what's what, and **Swear** tells you where it is.

Swing: Watery exercise. Participants wear **Swing Trunks**.

Take Sages: Don't expect quick results.

Tale Tense: Ping-pong.

THIN KYLE CALLER MONOCLE. EUSTON OWE A MONOCLE. NIGH SKIRL - WADE BOUT TOUR FREE POUNDS LESSEN THIS UN !
WEEK'S EXCISE WOODEN DOOM BOTH KNEE ARM.
WENDY LASS SEIZE ZONE FEET?

Tall Deep Ends: Praps. On the other hand, praps not.

Tangle: South American dance. See also **Rumble.**

Tessa Strenff: Conflict and strife seldom raise their ugly heads in Bristle, but when they do we have a champion worthy of the occasion. Tessa Strenff has appeared so often that it is impossible to imagine a strike, a demonstration, or a municipal squabble being reported without her aid. 'The whole dispute' we have been told, time and time again, 'has turned into a Tessa Strenff.' After that the reporter gets bogged down in a lot of boring detail which we can safely ignore, knowing that as long as Tessa's on the scene nobody is likely to chicken out.

Thin Else: Shopkeeper's question. There is a floating population of rare characters who are found only in Bristle: Sam Witch, Mimi, Jiminez, Late Ron, Levi Loan, Holly Daze, Homer Bout, Bleed Nell, Bess Tie-Can, Ark Tim, Chuck Doubt and Wendy Lass, to name but a few. To these should be added Thin Else, found in every shop in the city. So important is her presence that she has become the official patron saint of retailing. Whenever a shopkeeper wants to make another sale, he stimulates the customer with the sacred words: **Thin Else**? The sainted Else rarely lets him down.

Timp Airs: Can of fruit.

Tint; Taint: Firm denials. Not quite as definite as **Snot**.

Toes Track: Device for keeping burnt bread cold at breakfast.

Tomb Mince: 120 seconds.

Tour Free: Less than 4.

Track Lice: Device for controlling cars and stuff at crossroads.

Tree Member: To bear in mind; as in: 'Few loss tit, sup chew to fine dit. Wear javit lass? Try tree member!'

Trite: Hard a starboard. Opposite of leftward.

Truss: Faith, confidence. Also used of charitable bodies, e.g. National Truss.

Tuthrend: Down thurr, not up yer.

Twinges: Short distance. See **Ninch**. Strictly speaking, Twinges is Ninch multiplied by two.

Twitch: Serious talk; as in: 'Is this the statement twitch you refer?'

Tzar Bull: Attractive; worth having but not at any price. See also **Ness Serry** and **Sensual**.

Usure Red: Think about it.

View Knee: Shopper's request; as in: 'View knee brockley today?'

Waddle: Request for advice; as in: 'Waddle-eye do? Scone midnight anny snot tome yet. Sun-like R Tom, stain out slates this.'

Waddle Eye Sate: See **Sup Chew Knit**.

Wafer: See **Ice Poseys**.

Wake Sup: Give me a shake.

Wane: Entrance.

War: Basic commodity, supplied by Bristle War Works. Unless heated, it is coal war.

Welt: Preliminary warning noise that a poor excuse is coming; as in: 'Welts never happened before.'

GUESS TUCK INTO IT, LAD! GHOST STRAY TED FORA MILE NAFF, ANNUAL REACH THE SIKH DEBTS. THEY'D BE MORON GREYFUL FOR SUMMON TWELP EM MARCH.
PHONEY I CUD BUY TIM...
BOOM!- BANGA! BOOM!!- BOOM!

Wendy Lass: Question of recent behaviour; as in: 'He looks Leica rub sheep. Wendy lass have a bath?'

Wessun: Bristle's answer to Majorca.

Wess Vinglun: The region around Bristle. There ia a University of the Wess Vinglun (formerly Sodding Chipbury Polytechnic).

Whiff: Opposite of length

Whirled A Good: Vast improvement.

Wide Jew?: What were your reasons?

Wide Wye?: Search for reason; as in: 'Surly! Wide wye after go to bed?'

Wife Runts: Male briefs.

Wimms Inns Toot: Militant female movement dedicated to fighting pollution, making jam, wearing hats, and singing *Jerusalem*.

Wine Chew?: A different search for reason; as in: 'Wine chew gopher a nice long walk?' The phrase is similar to **Wive View**, which itself is not to be confused with **Wive Alley**, a canyon separating England from Wales.

Wine Tea?: see **Dwight Elm Outer**.

Wodge: Opening word of cross-examination; as in: 'Wodge you mean bite?'

Wodge Yew Speck?: Challenge of expectations.

Woot Nun Dredge: Pleasant village at present to the north of Bristle, doomed one day to be absorbed by the city's sprawl unless somebody puts his foot down.

Wop Rices?: How much is?

Word: Anxious.

Work Knee; Work Nigh: Enquiries concerning whereabouts; for example:
'Work knee parky scar?'
'Work nigh see the prayed?'

Worm Stew: Further enquiry concerning whereabouts; for example:
A. 'Pretty ice lated yer, incher? Worms stew gopher yer gross rees?'
B. 'Bout mile naff, ice pose. Mine jew, the misses bake slot.'

Worse: Term used in interrogation concerning whereabouts. **Worse** is a prime example of the beauty and economy of speech in Bristle. Elsewhere it takes three words (Where have you? or Where has it?) to convey the meaning that Worse contains in one taut syllable. It figures largely in Bristle's day-to-day conversation. Examples are: **Worse Bin**? and **Worse Tall Gone**?

Woss: Term used in interrogation concerning property. This is another example of the admirable brevity of Bristle. **Woss** does the work of What do you? or What have you? Examples are: **Woss Sink**? (What is your opinion?) And **Woss Scot**? (What have you acquired?).

Wreck Knits: The act of estimating or calculating; as in:
Motorist: Sport Zed long yer, den?
Pedestrian: R. Wreck knits bout mile naff, stray ted.

Wreck Nigh: Statement of belief, as in: 'Wreck nigh can park here. Sony double yellow lines.'

Wreck Ross: International disaster-relief agency.

Y Tree: Notorious roundabout between Red Lun and Wesbree.

Yearn: Two meanings: (1) As part of the phrase 'Yearn Thurr', meaning 'scattered about.' (2) By itself, meaning 'the ability to hear'; as in: 'Lav to shout – ease ardour yearn.'

Yerp: The Continent.

Yukon Talk: You're no better.

Yule Laughter: Opening words of command or requirement; as in: 'Yule laughter buyer summit – aft trawl, sir birthday.' See also **Dummy**.

Yuma: Fun or amusement; as in: 'Censor Yuma'. Also lead-in to descriptive remark, such as: 'Yuma secker tree yer, incher?' or 'Yuma lines wine!'

WODGE YEW FRIDAYS EGG SIN? MOAT ROYAL?
CAR NECKS PECKED MEATER DOOM PROP LEA LONG SHORE FIRES PORN OUT SMOKE.
STANS TREASON.

Yer! Payer tension! This
STIFF CUT
is awarded to
....
because he/she is
100% BRISTLE
and you'd better believe me
or diesel get my fist up thy frote.
Grace Tepp-Ford
Bristle's First Lady

Historical Bristle

Queen Victoria; College Green

Cloaked Horseman; Lewins Mead

Memorial to John Cabot, discoverer of America in 1497; Narrow Quay

William Tyndale, first to translate the Bible into English; Millennium Square

Cary Grant; Millennium Square

Apotheosis of Sabrina, Goddess of the Severn; Broad Quay

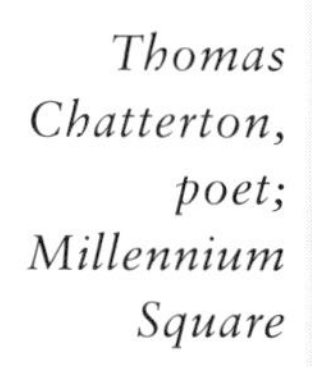

Thomas Chatterton, poet; Millennium Square

Rajah Rammohun Roy, Philosopher, Reformer, Patriot, Scholar; Central Library, College Green

John Wesley; Broadmead

Edward Colston, M.P., Colston Avenue

Gloucestershire Regiment Boer War Memorial, Queen's Road

William III, Queen Square

Edmund Burke, M.P., Colston Avenue

Samuel Morley, M.P.
Lewins Mead